40 Rice Recipes for Home

By: Kelly Johnson

Table of Contents

- Fried Rice
- Risotto
- Paella
- Pilaf
- Jollof Rice
- Sushi Rice
- Arroz con Pollo
- Biryani
- Rice Pudding
- Lemon Rice
- Coconut Rice
- Spanish Rice
- Rice and Beans
- Khichdi
- Stuffed Bell Peppers with Rice
- Sweet Rice with Cinnamon
- Teriyaki Rice
- Greek Lemon Rice
- Rice Salad
- Mushroom Risotto
- Cajun Rice
- Tomato Rice
- Wild Rice Soup
- Chicken and Rice Casserole
- Yellow Rice
- Beef Stroganoff with Rice
- Thai Pineapple Fried Rice
- Garlic Rice
- Tandoori Rice
- Moroccan Rice
- Egg Fried Rice
- Herb Rice

- Sesame Rice
- Creamy Rice and Spinach
- Rice and Lentils
- Black Bean Rice
- Basmati Rice with Cardamom
- Rice and Shrimp
- Asian Rice Noodles
- Rice and Chickpeas

Fried Rice

- 2 cups cooked jasmine or long-grain rice (preferably cold)
- 2 tbsp vegetable oil
- 1 small onion, finely chopped
- 2 cloves garlic, minced
- 1 cup mixed vegetables (carrots, peas, corn)
- 2 large eggs, beaten
- 1 cup cooked chicken, shrimp, or pork (optional)
- 3 tbsp soy sauce
- 1 tbsp oyster sauce (optional)
- 2 green onions, chopped
- Salt and pepper to taste

Instructions:

1. **Heat Oil:** In a large skillet or wok, heat vegetable oil over medium-high heat.
2. **Sauté Aromatics:** Add onion and garlic, and cook until translucent.
3. **Cook Vegetables:** Add mixed vegetables and cook until tender.
4. **Add Eggs:** Push vegetables to one side, pour beaten eggs into the pan, and scramble until fully cooked.
5. **Combine Ingredients:** Add the cold rice, cooked meat (if using), soy sauce, and oyster sauce. Stir-fry everything together until well mixed and heated through.
6. **Season:** Add green onions, salt, and pepper to taste.
7. **Serve:** Serve hot, garnished with additional green onions if desired.

Risotto

- 1 1/2 cups Arborio rice
- 4 cups chicken or vegetable broth
- 1 cup dry white wine
- 1 small onion, finely chopped
- 2 cloves garlic, minced
- 2 tbsp olive oil
- 1/2 cup grated Parmesan cheese
- 2 tbsp butter
- Salt and pepper to taste
- Fresh herbs (optional, for garnish)

Instructions:

1. **Warm Broth:** In a saucepan, keep the broth warm over low heat.
2. **Sauté Aromatics:** In a large pan, heat olive oil over medium heat. Add onion and garlic, and cook until translucent.
3. **Cook Rice:** Add Arborio rice and cook for 2 minutes, stirring frequently.
4. **Add Wine:** Pour in the wine and cook until it has mostly evaporated.
5. **Add Broth Gradually:** Start adding warm broth, one ladleful at a time, stirring constantly. Allow each addition to be absorbed before adding more broth. Continue until the rice is creamy and tender (about 18-20 minutes).
6. **Finish:** Stir in Parmesan cheese and butter. Season with salt and pepper.
7. **Serve:** Garnish with fresh herbs if desired and serve immediately.

Paella

- 2 tbsp olive oil
- 1 onion, chopped
- 3 cloves garlic, minced
- 1 bell pepper, chopped
- 1 cup tomatoes, chopped
- 1 1/2 cups short-grain rice (such as Bomba or Arborio)
- 3 cups chicken or seafood broth
- 1/2 tsp saffron threads
- 1 tsp smoked paprika
- 1 cup cooked chicken, diced
- 1 cup seafood (such as shrimp, mussels, and clams)
- 1 cup peas
- 1 lemon, cut into wedges
- Salt and pepper to taste
- Fresh parsley, chopped (for garnish)

Instructions:

1. **Heat Oil:** In a large paella pan or skillet, heat olive oil over medium heat.
2. **Sauté Aromatics:** Add onion, garlic, and bell pepper, and cook until softened.
3. **Add Tomatoes and Spices:** Stir in tomatoes, saffron, and smoked paprika. Cook for a few minutes.
4. **Add Rice:** Add the rice and stir to coat it with the tomato mixture.
5. **Add Broth:** Pour in the broth and bring to a simmer. Do not stir after this point.
6. **Add Proteins:** Arrange chicken, seafood, and peas on top of the rice. Cover and simmer until the rice is tender and the liquid is absorbed (about 20-25 minutes).
7. **Serve:** Garnish with lemon wedges and fresh parsley. Serve hot.

Pilaf

- 1 1/2 cups long-grain rice
- 2 tbsp butter or olive oil
- 1 onion, chopped
- 2 cloves garlic, minced
- 3 cups chicken or vegetable broth
- 1/4 cup slivered almonds (optional)
- 1/4 cup dried raisins or currants (optional)
- Salt and pepper to taste

Instructions:

1. **Heat Butter:** In a large pot, heat butter or olive oil over medium heat.
2. **Sauté Aromatics:** Add onion and garlic, and cook until translucent.
3. **Add Rice:** Stir in the rice and cook for 2-3 minutes until slightly toasted.
4. **Add Broth:** Pour in the broth and bring to a boil. Reduce heat to low, cover, and simmer for 15-20 minutes until the rice is tender and the liquid is absorbed.
5. **Finish:** Stir in slivered almonds and raisins if using. Season with salt and pepper.
6. **Serve:** Fluff with a fork before serving.

Jollof Rice

- 2 cups long-grain parboiled rice
- 1/4 cup vegetable oil
- 1 onion, chopped
- 3 cloves garlic, minced
- 1 bell pepper, chopped
- 1 cup tomato paste
- 1 cup chicken or vegetable broth
- 1 tsp paprika
- 1/2 tsp thyme
- 1/2 tsp curry powder
- 1 bay leaf
- Salt and pepper to taste
- 1 cup mixed vegetables (carrots, peas, green beans)

Instructions:

1. **Heat Oil:** In a large pot, heat vegetable oil over medium heat.
2. **Sauté Aromatics:** Add onion, garlic, and bell pepper, and cook until softened.
3. **Add Tomato Paste and Spices:** Stir in tomato paste, paprika, thyme, curry powder, and bay leaf. Cook for a few minutes.
4. **Add Rice and Broth:** Stir in the rice and mix well with the tomato mixture. Pour in the broth and bring to a boil.
5. **Simmer:** Reduce heat to low, cover, and simmer for 20-25 minutes until the rice is cooked and the liquid is absorbed.
6. **Add Vegetables:** Stir in mixed vegetables during the last 10 minutes of cooking.
7. **Serve:** Fluff with a fork and serve hot.

Sushi Rice

- 2 cups sushi rice
- 2 cups water
- 1/2 cup rice vinegar
- 1/4 cup granulated sugar
- 1/2 tsp salt

Instructions:

1. **Rinse Rice:** Rinse sushi rice under cold water until the water runs clear.
2. **Cook Rice:** Combine rice and water in a rice cooker or pot. Cook according to the rice cooker instructions or bring to a boil, then cover and reduce heat to low. Simmer for 18-20 minutes.
3. **Prepare Seasoning:** In a small saucepan, heat rice vinegar, sugar, and salt until dissolved. Do not boil.
4. **Season Rice:** Transfer cooked rice to a large bowl. Gently fold in the vinegar mixture while the rice is still warm.
5. **Cool:** Let rice cool to room temperature before using for sushi.

Arroz con Pollo

- 2 tbsp vegetable oil
- 4 chicken thighs, bone-in and skinless
- 1 onion, chopped
- 3 cloves garlic, minced
- 1 bell pepper, chopped
- 1 cup tomatoes, chopped
- 1 1/2 cups long-grain rice
- 2 cups chicken broth
- 1/2 tsp saffron threads
- 1/2 tsp paprika
- 1/2 tsp cumin
- 1 cup peas
- 1/2 cup olives (optional)
- Salt and pepper to taste

Instructions:

1. **Brown Chicken:** Heat vegetable oil in a large pot over medium heat. Brown the chicken on all sides and set aside.
2. **Sauté Aromatics:** In the same pot, add onion, garlic, and bell pepper, and cook until softened.
3. **Add Tomatoes and Spices:** Stir in tomatoes, saffron, paprika, and cumin. Cook for a few minutes.
4. **Add Rice and Broth:** Stir in the rice, then add chicken broth. Bring to a boil.
5. **Combine Chicken:** Return the chicken to the pot. Reduce heat to low, cover, and simmer for 30-35 minutes until the rice is tender and the chicken is cooked through.
6. **Finish:** Stir in peas and olives if using. Season with salt and pepper.
7. **Serve:** Fluff rice before serving.

Rice Pudding

- 1 cup short-grain rice
- 4 cups whole milk
- 1/2 cup granulated sugar
- 1/4 cup light brown sugar
- 1/4 tsp salt
- 1/2 tsp vanilla extract
- 1/2 tsp ground cinnamon
- 1/4 cup raisins (optional)

Instructions:

1. **Cook Rice:** In a large saucepan, combine rice and 1 cup of milk. Bring to a boil, then reduce heat and simmer for 15 minutes until the rice is tender.
2. **Add Remaining Ingredients:** Stir in remaining milk, granulated sugar, brown sugar, and salt. Cook over medium heat, stirring frequently, until the mixture thickens (about 20-25 minutes).
3. **Finish:** Remove from heat and stir in vanilla extract, ground cinnamon, and raisins if using.
4. **Serve:** Let cool slightly before serving warm or chilled.

Lemon Rice

- 2 cups long-grain rice
- 2 tbsp vegetable oil
- 1 tsp mustard seeds
- 1/2 tsp turmeric powder
- 1/2 tsp cumin seeds
- 1 green chili, chopped
- 1/4 cup peanuts
- 1/4 cup fresh lemon juice
- 2 tbsp fresh cilantro, chopped
- Salt to taste

Instructions:

1. **Cook Rice:** Prepare rice according to package instructions and let it cool.
2. **Heat Oil:** In a large pan, heat oil over medium heat. Add mustard seeds, cumin seeds, and green chili. Cook until the mustard seeds start popping.
3. **Add Spices and Peanuts:** Stir in turmeric powder and peanuts, and cook for another minute.
4. **Combine Rice:** Add the cooled rice to the pan and mix well.
5. **Add Lemon Juice:** Stir in lemon juice and salt. Cook for a few more minutes until heated through.
6. **Finish:** Garnish with fresh cilantro before serving.

Coconut Rice

- 1 cup jasmine or long-grain rice
- 1 cup coconut milk
- 1 cup water
- 1 tbsp sugar
- 1/2 tsp salt
- 1/4 cup shredded coconut (optional)

Instructions:

1. **Combine Ingredients:** In a medium pot, combine rice, coconut milk, water, sugar, and salt.
2. **Cook Rice:** Bring to a boil, then reduce heat to low. Cover and simmer for 18-20 minutes until the rice is tender and the liquid is absorbed.
3. **Finish:** Fluff with a fork and stir in shredded coconut if using. Serve warm.

Spanish Rice

- 2 tbsp vegetable oil
- 1 cup long-grain rice
- 1 small onion, chopped
- 2 cloves garlic, minced
- 1 can (14.5 oz) diced tomatoes
- 1 cup chicken broth
- 1/2 tsp chili powder
- 1/2 tsp paprika
- 1/2 tsp cumin
- Salt to taste

Instructions:

1. **Heat Oil:** In a large skillet, heat oil over medium heat. Add rice and cook, stirring frequently, until lightly toasted.
2. **Add Aromatics:** Add onion and garlic, and cook until softened.
3. **Add Tomatoes and Spices:** Stir in diced tomatoes, chili powder, paprika, cumin, and salt.
4. **Add Broth:** Pour in chicken broth and bring to a boil.
5. **Simmer:** Reduce heat to low, cover, and simmer for 20-25 minutes until the rice is tender and the liquid is absorbed.
6. **Serve:** Fluff with a fork before serving.

Rice and Beans

- 1 cup long-grain rice
- 1 can (15 oz) black beans or kidney beans, drained and rinsed
- 1 tbsp vegetable oil
- 1 small onion, chopped
- 2 cloves garlic, minced
- 1 bell pepper, chopped
- 1 cup chicken or vegetable broth
- 1 tsp cumin
- 1/2 tsp paprika
- Salt and pepper to taste

Instructions:

1. **Heat Oil:** In a large pot, heat oil over medium heat. Add onion, garlic, and bell pepper, and cook until softened.
2. **Add Rice and Spices:** Stir in rice, cumin, paprika, salt, and pepper. Cook for 1-2 minutes.
3. **Add Beans and Broth:** Pour in beans and broth. Bring to a boil.
4. **Simmer:** Reduce heat to low, cover, and simmer for 20-25 minutes until the rice is tender and the liquid is absorbed.
5. **Serve:** Fluff with a fork before serving.

Khichdi

- 1 cup basmati rice
- 1/2 cup split yellow moong dal (lentils)
- 2 tbsp vegetable oil
- 1 tsp cumin seeds
- 1/2 tsp turmeric powder
- 1/2 tsp ginger, minced
- 1 small onion, chopped
- 1 small tomato, chopped
- 1 cup mixed vegetables (carrots, peas, beans)
- 4 cups water
- Salt to taste

Instructions:

1. **Prepare Rice and Dal:** Rinse rice and moong dal under cold water.
2. **Heat Oil:** In a large pot, heat oil over medium heat. Add cumin seeds and cook until they start to sizzle.
3. **Add Aromatics:** Stir in turmeric, ginger, onion, and tomato. Cook until the onion is translucent.
4. **Add Vegetables and Rice:** Add mixed vegetables, rice, and dal. Stir well.
5. **Add Water and Simmer:** Pour in water and salt. Bring to a boil, then reduce heat to low. Cover and simmer for 20-25 minutes until the rice and dal are tender.
6. **Serve:** Fluff with a fork and serve hot.

Stuffed Bell Peppers with Rice

- 4 bell peppers (any color)
- 1 cup cooked rice
- 1/2 lb ground beef or turkey
- 1/2 cup onion, chopped
- 1 cup tomatoes, chopped
- 1/2 cup shredded cheese (optional)
- 1 tsp Italian seasoning
- Salt and pepper to taste

Instructions:

1. **Preheat Oven:** Preheat your oven to 375°F (190°C).
2. **Prepare Peppers:** Cut the tops off the bell peppers and remove seeds and membranes.
3. **Cook Meat:** In a skillet, cook ground beef or turkey with onion until browned. Drain excess fat.
4. **Combine Ingredients:** Stir in cooked rice, tomatoes, Italian seasoning, salt, and pepper. Cook for 5 minutes.
5. **Stuff Peppers:** Spoon the mixture into the bell peppers. Place peppers upright in a baking dish.
6. **Add Cheese:** Top with shredded cheese if desired.
7. **Bake:** Cover with foil and bake for 30-35 minutes. Remove foil and bake for an additional 5-10 minutes, until peppers are tender and cheese is melted. Serve hot.

Sweet Rice with Cinnamon

- 1 cup short-grain rice
- 2 cups whole milk
- 1/2 cup granulated sugar
- 1/4 tsp salt
- 1/2 tsp ground cinnamon
- 1/4 tsp vanilla extract

Instructions:

1. **Cook Rice:** In a large saucepan, combine rice and 1 cup of milk. Bring to a boil, reduce heat, and simmer for 15 minutes until rice is tender.
2. **Add Ingredients:** Stir in the remaining milk, sugar, and salt. Cook over medium heat, stirring occasionally, until thickened (about 20 minutes).
3. **Finish:** Remove from heat and stir in cinnamon and vanilla extract.
4. **Serve:** Serve warm or chilled.

Teriyaki Rice

- 2 cups jasmine rice
- 1/4 cup teriyaki sauce
- 2 cups water
- 1 tbsp vegetable oil
- 1 clove garlic, minced
- 1/2 cup chopped green onions

Instructions:

1. **Cook Rice:** Rinse rice under cold water. In a pot, combine rice and water. Bring to a boil, reduce heat to low, cover, and cook for 18-20 minutes until rice is tender.
2. **Prepare Teriyaki Mixture:** In a small pan, heat vegetable oil and sauté garlic until fragrant. Stir in teriyaki sauce.
3. **Combine:** Fluff the rice and mix in the teriyaki sauce and green onions.
4. **Serve:** Serve warm as a side dish.

Greek Lemon Rice

- 2 cups long-grain rice
- 2 cups chicken or vegetable broth
- 1/4 cup lemon juice
- 2 tbsp olive oil
- 1 small onion, chopped
- 1 clove garlic, minced
- 1/4 cup chopped fresh parsley
- Salt and pepper to taste

Instructions:

1. **Sauté Aromatics:** In a large pot, heat olive oil over medium heat. Add onion and garlic and cook until translucent.
2. **Add Rice:** Stir in rice and cook for 2-3 minutes.
3. **Add Broth and Lemon Juice:** Pour in broth and lemon juice. Bring to a boil, then reduce heat to low, cover, and simmer for 18-20 minutes until the rice is tender and liquid is absorbed.
4. **Finish:** Stir in fresh parsley and season with salt and pepper.
5. **Serve:** Fluff with a fork before serving.

Rice Salad

- 2 cups cooked and cooled rice (any variety)
- 1 cup cherry tomatoes, halved
- 1/2 cup cucumber, diced
- 1/4 cup red onion, finely chopped
- 1/4 cup black olives, sliced
- 1/4 cup feta cheese, crumbled
- 3 tbsp olive oil
- 2 tbsp red wine vinegar
- 1 tsp dried oregano
- Salt and pepper to taste

Instructions:

1. **Combine Ingredients:** In a large bowl, mix together rice, cherry tomatoes, cucumber, red onion, olives, and feta cheese.
2. **Prepare Dressing:** In a small bowl, whisk together olive oil, red wine vinegar, oregano, salt, and pepper.
3. **Dress Salad:** Pour dressing over the rice mixture and toss to coat evenly.
4. **Serve:** Chill before serving, or serve at room temperature.

Mushroom Risotto

- 1 1/2 cups Arborio rice
- 4 cups chicken or vegetable broth
- 1 cup white wine
- 2 tbsp olive oil
- 1 small onion, finely chopped
- 2 cloves garlic, minced
- 2 cups mushrooms, sliced
- 1/2 cup grated Parmesan cheese
- 2 tbsp butter
- Salt and pepper to taste

Instructions:

1. **Warm Broth:** Keep broth warm in a separate pot.
2. **Cook Aromatics:** In a large pan, heat olive oil. Sauté onion and garlic until translucent.
3. **Add Mushrooms:** Stir in mushrooms and cook until tender.
4. **Cook Rice:** Add Arborio rice and cook, stirring constantly, for 2-3 minutes. Add wine and cook until mostly absorbed.
5. **Add Broth:** Begin adding warm broth one ladleful at a time, stirring frequently. Allow each addition to be absorbed before adding more broth. Continue until rice is creamy and tender (about 18-20 minutes).
6. **Finish:** Stir in Parmesan cheese and butter. Season with salt and pepper.
7. **Serve:** Serve immediately.

Cajun Rice

- 2 cups long-grain rice
- 2 cups chicken broth
- 1 tbsp Cajun seasoning
- 1 tbsp vegetable oil
- 1 small onion, chopped
- 1 bell pepper, chopped
- 2 cloves garlic, minced
- 1 cup cooked sausage, diced (optional)

Instructions:

1. **Sauté Aromatics:** In a large pan, heat vegetable oil. Add onion, bell pepper, and garlic, and cook until softened.
2. **Add Rice and Spices:** Stir in rice and Cajun seasoning. Cook for 2 minutes.
3. **Add Broth and Sausage:** Pour in chicken broth and add cooked sausage if using. Bring to a boil.
4. **Simmer:** Reduce heat to low, cover, and simmer for 20-25 minutes until rice is tender and liquid is absorbed.
5. **Serve:** Fluff with a fork before serving.

Tomato Rice

- 1 1/2 cups long-grain rice
- 1 can (14.5 oz) diced tomatoes
- 1 cup chicken or vegetable broth
- 1 small onion, chopped
- 2 cloves garlic, minced
- 1 tsp dried basil
- 1/2 tsp dried oregano
- 2 tbsp olive oil
- Salt and pepper to taste

Instructions:

1. **Sauté Aromatics:** In a large pot, heat olive oil. Add onion and garlic and cook until translucent.
2. **Add Tomatoes and Spices:** Stir in diced tomatoes, basil, oregano, salt, and pepper.
3. **Add Rice and Broth:** Stir in rice and chicken broth. Bring to a boil.
4. **Simmer:** Reduce heat to low, cover, and simmer for 20-25 minutes until rice is tender and the liquid is absorbed.
5. **Serve:** Fluff with a fork before serving.

Wild Rice Soup

- 1 cup wild rice
- 1 tbsp vegetable oil
- 1 small onion, chopped
- 2 cloves garlic, minced
- 3 carrots, diced
- 2 celery stalks, diced
- 6 cups chicken or vegetable broth
- 1 cup mushrooms, sliced
- 1/2 cup heavy cream
- 1 tsp dried thyme
- Salt and pepper to taste

Instructions:

1. **Cook Rice:** Cook wild rice according to package instructions and set aside.
2. **Sauté Aromatics:** In a large pot, heat vegetable oil. Add onion, garlic, carrots, and celery, and cook until softened.
3. **Add Broth and Mushrooms:** Stir in broth, mushrooms, and thyme. Bring to a boil.
4. **Simmer:** Reduce heat and simmer for 20 minutes until vegetables are tender.
5. **Add Rice and Cream:** Stir in cooked rice and heavy cream. Heat through and season with salt and pepper.
6. **Serve:** Serve hot.

Chicken and Rice Casserole

- 2 cups cooked rice
- 2 cups cooked, shredded chicken
- 1 can (10.5 oz) cream of chicken soup
- 1/2 cup sour cream
- 1 cup shredded cheddar cheese
- 1/2 cup chicken broth
- 1/2 cup frozen peas and carrots
- 1/2 tsp garlic powder
- 1/2 tsp onion powder
- Salt and pepper to taste
- 1/4 cup bread crumbs (optional)

Instructions:

1. **Preheat Oven:** Preheat oven to 350°F (175°C).
2. **Combine Ingredients:** In a large bowl, mix together cooked rice, shredded chicken, cream of chicken soup, sour cream, 1/2 cup cheese, chicken broth, peas and carrots, garlic powder, onion powder, salt, and pepper.
3. **Transfer to Dish:** Spoon mixture into a greased baking dish.
4. **Add Topping:** Sprinkle with remaining cheese and bread crumbs if using.
5. **Bake:** Bake for 25-30 minutes, or until bubbly and golden on top.

Yellow Rice

- 1 cup long-grain rice
- 2 cups chicken or vegetable broth
- 1/4 cup vegetable oil
- 1/2 tsp turmeric powder
- 1/2 tsp paprika
- 1/4 tsp cumin
- 1 small onion, chopped
- 2 cloves garlic, minced
- Salt to taste

Instructions:

1. **Sauté Aromatics:** In a medium pot, heat vegetable oil. Add onion and garlic, and cook until softened.
2. **Add Spices:** Stir in turmeric, paprika, and cumin.
3. **Add Rice:** Add rice and cook, stirring for 2-3 minutes.
4. **Add Broth:** Pour in the broth and bring to a boil.
5. **Simmer:** Reduce heat to low, cover, and simmer for 18-20 minutes until rice is tender and the liquid is absorbed.
6. **Serve:** Fluff with a fork before serving.

Beef Stroganoff with Rice

- 1 lb beef sirloin, thinly sliced
- 1 cup mushrooms, sliced
- 1 small onion, chopped
- 2 cloves garlic, minced
- 1 cup sour cream
- 1 cup beef broth
- 1 tbsp Dijon mustard
- 1 tbsp flour
- 2 tbsp vegetable oil
- 2 cups cooked rice
- Salt and pepper to taste

Instructions:

1. **Cook Beef:** In a skillet, heat vegetable oil over medium heat. Add beef and cook until browned. Remove from pan and set aside.
2. **Sauté Aromatics:** In the same skillet, add onions, garlic, and mushrooms. Cook until tender.
3. **Prepare Sauce:** Stir in flour and cook for 1 minute. Add beef broth and Dijon mustard, and bring to a simmer.
4. **Add Beef:** Return beef to the skillet and simmer for 5 minutes. Stir in sour cream and cook until heated through. Season with salt and pepper.
5. **Serve:** Spoon beef stroganoff over cooked rice.

Thai Pineapple Fried Rice

- 2 cups cooked jasmine rice (preferably cold)
- 1 cup pineapple chunks
- 2 tbsp vegetable oil
- 1/2 cup onion, chopped
- 2 cloves garlic, minced
- 1/2 cup bell pepper, diced
- 1/2 cup carrots, diced
- 2 eggs, lightly beaten
- 2 tbsp soy sauce
- 1 tbsp fish sauce
- 1/4 cup chopped fresh cilantro
- 1/4 cup chopped green onions

Instructions:

1. **Heat Oil:** In a large pan or wok, heat vegetable oil. Add onion, garlic, bell pepper, and carrots. Cook until vegetables are tender.
2. **Add Rice:** Stir in cooked rice and cook until heated through.
3. **Add Pineapple and Eggs:** Push rice to one side of the pan and scramble eggs in the empty side. Mix eggs into the rice.
4. **Season:** Add pineapple, soy sauce, and fish sauce. Stir well to combine.
5. **Finish:** Garnish with cilantro and green onions before serving.

Garlic Rice

- 2 cups jasmine rice
- 4 cloves garlic, minced
- 2 cups chicken or vegetable broth
- 2 tbsp vegetable oil
- 1/4 cup chopped parsley (optional)
- Salt to taste

Instructions:

1. **Sauté Garlic:** In a medium pot, heat vegetable oil over medium heat. Add garlic and cook until fragrant (about 1 minute).
2. **Add Rice:** Stir in rice and cook for 2-3 minutes.
3. **Add Broth:** Pour in the broth and bring to a boil.
4. **Simmer:** Reduce heat to low, cover, and simmer for 18-20 minutes until rice is tender and the liquid is absorbed.
5. **Finish:** Fluff with a fork and stir in chopped parsley if using. Season with salt.

Tandoori Rice

- 2 cups basmati rice
- 2 tbsp tandoori masala
- 2 cups water
- 1 tbsp vegetable oil
- 1/2 cup onion, chopped
- 2 cloves garlic, minced
- 1/2 cup chopped tomatoes
- Salt to taste

Instructions:

1. **Sauté Aromatics:** In a large pot, heat vegetable oil. Add onion and garlic, and cook until softened.
2. **Add Spices:** Stir in tandoori masala and cook for 1 minute.
3. **Add Rice and Tomatoes:** Stir in rice and chopped tomatoes. Cook for 2 minutes.
4. **Add Water:** Pour in water and bring to a boil.
5. **Simmer:** Reduce heat to low, cover, and simmer for 18-20 minutes until rice is tender and the liquid is absorbed.
6. **Serve:** Fluff with a fork before serving.

Moroccan Rice

- 1 cup basmati rice
- 1 cup chicken or vegetable broth
- 1/4 cup raisins
- 1/4 cup sliced almonds
- 1/2 tsp ground cumin
- 1/2 tsp ground cinnamon
- 2 tbsp olive oil
- 1 small onion, chopped
- Salt and pepper to taste

Instructions:

1. **Sauté Aromatics:** In a medium pot, heat olive oil over medium heat. Add onion and cook until translucent.
2. **Add Spices:** Stir in cumin and cinnamon.
3. **Add Rice:** Stir in rice and cook for 2 minutes.
4. **Add Broth and Raisins:** Pour in broth and add raisins. Bring to a boil.
5. **Simmer:** Reduce heat to low, cover, and simmer for 18-20 minutes until rice is tender and the liquid is absorbed.
6. **Finish:** Stir in sliced almonds before serving.

Egg Fried Rice

- 2 cups cooked jasmine rice (preferably cold)
- 2 eggs, lightly beaten
- 1/2 cup frozen peas and carrots
- 2 tbsp vegetable oil
- 2 cloves garlic, minced
- 2 tbsp soy sauce
- 1/4 cup chopped green onions

Instructions:

1. **Heat Oil:** In a large pan or wok, heat vegetable oil. Add garlic and cook until fragrant.
2. **Scramble Eggs:** Push garlic to one side of the pan, pour in beaten eggs, and scramble until cooked through.
3. **Add Vegetables:** Stir in peas and carrots and cook until tender.
4. **Add Rice:** Add cold rice and soy sauce. Stir well and cook until heated through.
5. **Finish:** Garnish with green onions before serving.

Herb Rice

- 1 cup long-grain rice
- 2 cups chicken or vegetable broth
- 2 tbsp olive oil
- 1 small onion, chopped
- 2 cloves garlic, minced
- 1/4 cup chopped fresh parsley
- 1/4 cup chopped fresh thyme
- 1/4 cup chopped fresh basil (optional)
- Salt and pepper to taste

Instructions:

1. **Sauté Aromatics:** In a medium pot, heat olive oil over medium heat. Add onion and garlic, and cook until softened.
2. **Add Rice:** Stir in rice and cook for 2-3 minutes.
3. **Add Broth:** Pour in broth and bring to a boil.
4. **Simmer:** Reduce heat to low, cover, and simmer for 18-20 minutes until rice is tender and the liquid is absorbed.
5. **Finish:** Stir in chopped herbs, and season with salt and pepper. Fluff with a fork before serving.

Sesame Rice

- 1 cup jasmine or long-grain rice
- 2 cups water
- 2 tbsp sesame oil
- 2 tbsp soy sauce
- 1 tbsp sesame seeds (toasted)
- 2 green onions, chopped

Instructions:

1. **Cook Rice:** Rinse rice under cold water. In a pot, combine rice and water. Bring to a boil, reduce heat to low, cover, and cook for 18-20 minutes until rice is tender.
2. **Prepare Seasoning:** In a small bowl, mix sesame oil and soy sauce.
3. **Combine:** Fluff the rice and stir in sesame oil mixture.
4. **Finish:** Sprinkle with toasted sesame seeds and chopped green onions before serving.

Creamy Rice and Spinach

- 1 cup Arborio rice
- 2 cups chicken or vegetable broth
- 1/2 cup heavy cream
- 2 cups fresh spinach, chopped
- 1 small onion, chopped
- 2 cloves garlic, minced
- 1/2 cup grated Parmesan cheese
- 2 tbsp olive oil
- Salt and pepper to taste

Instructions:

1. **Sauté Aromatics:** In a large pot, heat olive oil over medium heat. Add onion and garlic, and cook until translucent.
2. **Cook Rice:** Stir in Arborio rice and cook for 2-3 minutes.
3. **Add Broth:** Begin adding warm broth one ladleful at a time, stirring frequently. Allow each addition to be absorbed before adding more. Continue until rice is creamy and tender (about 18-20 minutes).
4. **Add Spinach and Cream:** Stir in chopped spinach and heavy cream. Cook until spinach is wilted and cream is heated through.
5. **Finish:** Stir in Parmesan cheese, and season with salt and pepper. Serve immediately.

Rice and Lentils

- 1 cup basmati rice
- 1/2 cup brown or green lentils
- 2 cups vegetable or chicken broth
- 1 small onion, chopped
- 2 cloves garlic, minced
- 1/2 tsp cumin
- 1/2 tsp paprika
- 1/4 tsp turmeric
- 2 tbsp olive oil
- Salt and pepper to taste

Instructions:

1. **Cook Lentils:** In a medium pot, combine lentils and 2 cups of water. Bring to a boil, then reduce heat and simmer for 20 minutes until tender. Drain and set aside.
2. **Sauté Aromatics:** In a large pot, heat olive oil over medium heat. Add onion and garlic, and cook until softened.
3. **Add Spices:** Stir in cumin, paprika, and turmeric.
4. **Cook Rice:** Add rice and cook for 2 minutes. Pour in broth and bring to a boil.
5. **Simmer:** Reduce heat to low, cover, and simmer for 18-20 minutes until rice is tender and the liquid is absorbed.
6. **Combine:** Stir in cooked lentils, and season with salt and pepper. Fluff with a fork before serving.

Black Bean Rice

- 1 cup long-grain rice
- 1 can (15 oz) black beans, drained and rinsed
- 2 cups chicken or vegetable broth
- 1 small onion, chopped
- 2 cloves garlic, minced
- 1/2 cup bell pepper, diced
- 1 tsp cumin
- 1/2 tsp chili powder
- 2 tbsp vegetable oil
- Salt and pepper to taste
- 1/4 cup chopped fresh cilantro (optional)

Instructions:

1. **Sauté Aromatics:** In a large pot, heat vegetable oil over medium heat. Add onion, garlic, and bell pepper, and cook until softened.
2. **Add Spices:** Stir in cumin and chili powder.
3. **Add Rice:** Add rice and cook for 2 minutes.
4. **Add Broth:** Pour in broth and bring to a boil.
5. **Simmer:** Reduce heat to low, cover, and simmer for 18-20 minutes until rice is tender and the liquid is absorbed.
6. **Add Beans:** Stir in black beans and cook until heated through. Season with salt and pepper.
7. **Finish:** Garnish with chopped cilantro if desired. Fluff with a fork before serving.

Basmati Rice with Cardamom

- 1 cup basmati rice
- 2 cups water
- 4 green cardamom pods
- 2 tbsp ghee or vegetable oil
- 1 small onion, chopped (optional)
- Salt to taste

Instructions:

1. **Rinse Rice:** Rinse basmati rice under cold water until water runs clear.
2. **Sauté Aromatics (Optional):** In a medium pot, heat ghee or vegetable oil. Add onion if using, and cook until translucent.
3. **Add Cardamom:** Stir in cardamom pods and cook for 1 minute.
4. **Cook Rice:** Add rice and cook for 2-3 minutes, stirring to coat with oil.
5. **Add Water and Simmer:** Pour in water and bring to a boil. Reduce heat to low, cover, and simmer for 18-20 minutes until rice is tender and the liquid is absorbed.
6. **Finish:** Fluff rice with a fork and discard cardamom pods before serving.

Rice and Shrimp

- 1 cup jasmine rice
- 1 cup shrimp, peeled and deveined
- 2 cups chicken or vegetable broth
- 1 small onion, chopped
- 2 cloves garlic, minced
- 1/2 cup bell pepper, diced
- 1/2 tsp paprika
- 1/2 tsp dried oregano
- 2 tbsp vegetable oil
- Salt and pepper to taste
- 2 tbsp chopped fresh parsley (optional)

Instructions:

1. **Sauté Aromatics:** In a large pot, heat vegetable oil. Add onion, garlic, and bell pepper, and cook until softened.
2. **Add Spices and Rice:** Stir in paprika and oregano, then add rice and cook for 2 minutes.
3. **Add Broth:** Pour in broth and bring to a boil.
4. **Simmer Rice:** Reduce heat to low, cover, and simmer for 15 minutes.
5. **Add Shrimp:** Stir in shrimp, cover, and cook for an additional 5-7 minutes until shrimp is cooked and rice is tender.
6. **Finish:** Season with salt and pepper, and garnish with chopped parsley if desired.

Asian Rice Noodles

- 8 oz rice noodles
- 2 tbsp vegetable oil
- 1 cup bell pepper, sliced
- 1 cup snap peas
- 1 small onion, sliced
- 2 cloves garlic, minced
- 3 tbsp soy sauce
- 1 tbsp hoisin sauce
- 1 tsp sesame oil
- 2 green onions, sliced
- Sesame seeds (optional)

Instructions:

1. **Cook Noodles:** Cook rice noodles according to package instructions. Drain and set aside.
2. **Sauté Vegetables:** In a large pan or wok, heat vegetable oil. Add onion, garlic, bell pepper, and snap peas. Cook until vegetables are tender-crisp.
3. **Add Sauces:** Stir in soy sauce, hoisin sauce, and sesame oil.
4. **Combine:** Add cooked noodles to the pan and toss to combine with the sauce and vegetables.
5. **Finish:** Garnish with sliced green onions and sesame seeds before serving.

Rice and Chickpeas

- 1 cup basmati rice
- 1 can (15 oz) chickpeas, drained and rinsed
- 2 cups vegetable broth
- 1 small onion, chopped
- 2 cloves garlic, minced
- 1/2 tsp cumin
- 1/2 tsp coriander
- 1/2 tsp turmeric
- 2 tbsp olive oil
- Salt and pepper to taste
- 1/4 cup chopped fresh cilantro (optional)

Instructions:

1. **Sauté Aromatics:** In a large pot, heat olive oil. Add onion and garlic, and cook until softened.
2. **Add Spices:** Stir in cumin, coriander, and turmeric, and cook for 1 minute.
3. **Add Rice:** Stir in rice and cook for 2 minutes.
4. **Add Broth and Chickpeas:** Pour in broth and add chickpeas. Bring to a boil.
5. **Simmer:** Reduce heat to low, cover, and simmer for 18-20 minutes until rice is tender and the liquid is absorbed.
6. **Finish:** Season with salt and pepper, and garnish with chopped cilantro if desired. Fluff with a fork before serving.

www.ingramcontent.com/pod-product-compliance
Lightning Source LLC
LaVergne TN
LVHW081510060526
838201LV00056BA/3034